DO YOU REALLY WANT TO

VISIT A TEMPERATE FOREST?

WRITTEN BY BRIDGET HEOS · ILLUSTRATED BY DANIELE FABBRI

Amicus Illustrated is published by Amicus
P.O. Box 1329, Mankato, MN 56002
www.amicuspublishing.us

Library of Congress Cataloging-in-Publication Data
Heos, Bridget.
 Do you really want to visit a temperate forest? /
Bridget Heos; illustrated by Daniele Fabbri.
   pages cm
 Includes bibliographical references and index.
 Summary: "A child goes on an adventure to three types of
forests in North America, discovering what the climate is
like and the animals and plants that make their homes in
different parts of the forest biome. Includes world map of
temperate forests and glossary"— Provided by publisher.
 ISBN 978-1-60753-451-8 (library binding: alk. paper) —
ISBN 978-1-60753-666-6 (ebook)
 1. Forest ecology—Juvenile literature. 2. Forests and
forestry—North America—Juvenile literature. I. Fabbri,
Daniele, 1978- illustrator. II. Title.
QH541.5.F6H465 2015
577.3—dc23   2013029101

Editor: Rebecca Glaser
Designer: Kathleen Petelinsek

Printed in the United States of America at
Corporate Graphics in North Mankato, Minnesota.
10 9 8 7 6 5 4 3 2 1

ABOUT THE AUTHOR

Bridget Heos is the author of more than 60 books for children, including many Amicus Illustrated titles and her recent picture book *Mustache Baby* (Houghton Mifflin Harcourt, 2013). She lives on the prairie of Kansas City with her husband and four children.

ABOUT THE ILLUSTRATOR

Daniele Fabbri was born in Ravenna, Italy, in 1978. He graduated from Istituto Europeo di Design in Milan, Italy, and started his career as a cartoon animator, storyboarder, and background designer for animated series. He has worked as a freelance illustrator since 2003, collaborating with international publishers and advertising agencies.

So you want to visit a forest? True, they are like something out of a fairy tale. But people get eaten by wolves in fairy tales!

Don't worry. You're off to a real forest in the Pacific Northwest. The largest temperate forest in the world, it spans from Alaska to California. Do you have tree-climbing gear?

You'll also need hiking boots and rain gear. The Pacific Northwest is a temperate *rain*forest. It gets more than 47 inches (120 cm) of rain per year.

First stop: Washington state. Bundle up! Temperate rainforests stay cool year round. Conifers—trees with needles and cones—cover this land.

Why does it rain so much here? When wet ocean
air collides with mountains to the east, it rains.

Oh no! Too much rain can cause a landslide.
Landslides can wipe out trees. Timber!

Fallen trees become part of the forest floor. Mosses grow on them. Trees sprout up. These logs are called nurse logs. They also shelter insects, birds, and small critters. What do they need shelter from?

The big bad wolf!
Wolves aren't really
bad, but they are big.
And they are predators.
They hunt other animals
to eat. And according to
fairy tales, they like
red hoods. Uh-oh!

Of course, fairy tales aren't real. Wolves don't normally attack people. And keep in mind: wolves do not climb trees.

Are *you* ready to climb? Say hello to the treetops, or forest canopy. You'll see more sunlight and different animals.

Now ride the zip line from tree to tree. What if you could zip all the way to California?

You could visit Redwood National Park and the world's tallest trees. Some of these trees are 2,000 years old. The tallest one is 379.1 feet (115.55 m)—taller than a 37-story skyscraper.

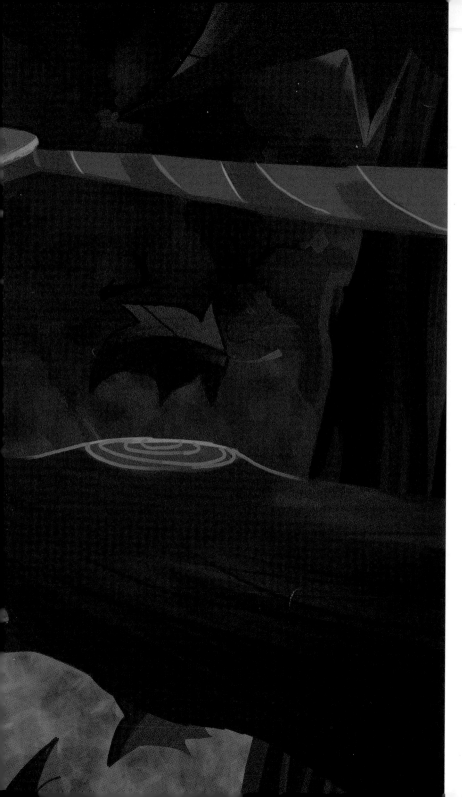

What if you could zip all the way across America to the *Northeast?* In the Adirondack Forest in New York, the summers are warm and winters are cold. This is a temperate forest. It rains (and snows), but not as much as in a temperate rainforest. Many of the trees are deciduous. In fall, their leaves turn colors and fall off.

The leaves blanket the forest floor. Insects live underneath.
Animals eat the insects. They also eat nuts and acorns from the trees.

And this black bear eats delicious berries from a shrub.

Bears can climb. Give it space. Back away slowly. If it comes closer, make noise. Once it knows you are human, it will probably go away. Bear attacks are rare.

Look! Here is a shelter for you.
And they left behind some porridge!

TEMPERATE FORESTS OF THE WORLD
(INCLUDES TEMPERATE RAINFORESTS)

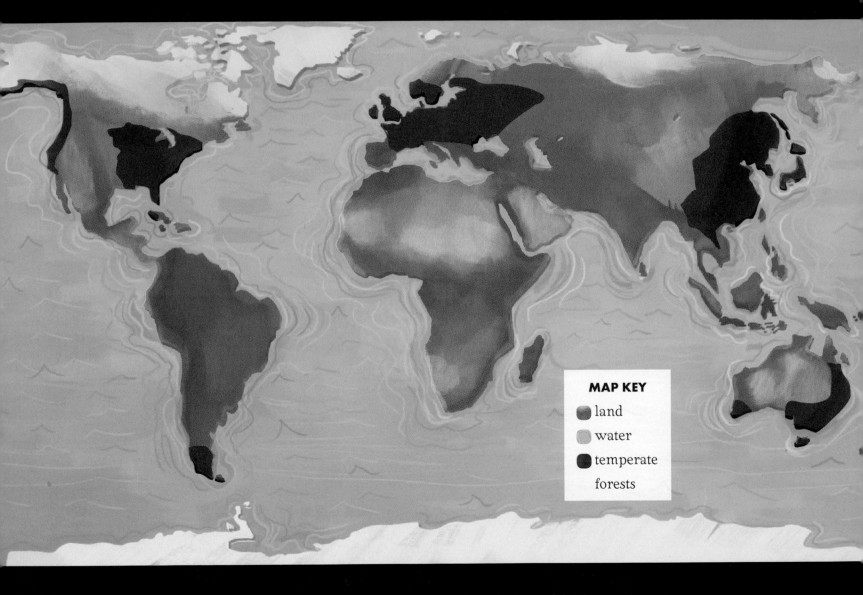

MAP KEY
- land
- water
- temperate forests

SAVE THE FORESTS

People have already chopped down half of the world's forests. Forests are good for the earth. They provide homes to plants and animals. Here are some ways you can save them:

- Recycle paper and use recycled paper.

- Visit forests and learn more about them.

- Contact your government representatives about conserving forest lands.

GLOSSARY

canopy The treetop area of a forest.

conifer An evergreen tree that produces pinecones.

deciduous tree A tree that sheds its leaves every year.

nurse log A fallen tree on which new trees grow.

predator An animal that hunts and eats other animals.

temperate forest A forest (rainforest or not) in cooler climates.

temperate rainforest A rainforest that averages more than 47 inches (120 cm) of rain per year and with average temperatures below 60°F (16°C) in July.

tree-climbing gear Equipment, including helmets, ropes, and harnesses, that support people while they climb or zip line between trees.

zip line A rope running between two trees so a person can slide from one end of the rope to the other.

READ MORE

Amstutz, Lisa J. **What Eats What in a Forest Food Chain?** North Mankato, Minn.: Picture Window Books, 2013.

Benoit, Peter. **Temperate Forests**. New York: Children's Press, 2011.

Hurtig, Jennifer. **Deciduous Forests**. New York: AV2 by Weigl, 2012.

Newland, Sonya. **Woodland and Forest Animals**. Mankato, Minn.: Smart Apple Media, 2012.

WEBSITES

Discover the Forest
http://www.discovertheforest.org/
Find ideas for exploring forests, with tips for what to bring and what to do while you explore.

The Life of a Tree
http://www.arborday.org/kids/carly/lifeofatree/
Learn about how trees grow.

Redwoods Learning Center
http://education.savetheredwoods.org/kit/index.php
Learn more about the world's tallest trees, the redwoods.

What's it Like Where You Live?: Temperate Deciduous Forest Topics
http://www.mbgnet.net/sets/temp
View photos and read about how forest plants and animals adapt to the changing seasons.

Every effort has been made to ensure that these websites are appropriate for children. However, because of the nature of the Internet, it is impossible to guarantee that these sites will remain active indefinitely or that their contents will not be altered.